Copyright © 2023 by Summer Collins
All rights reserved. This book or any portion thereof
may not be reproduced or used in any manner whatsoever
without the express written permission of the publisher
except for the use of brief quotations in a book review.
Printed in the United States of America.
First Printing, 2023
ISBN 979-8-218-32604-3
Kindle Direct Publishing

For Mikel,

the most beautiful stranger I'd ever seen,

and the only thing that's changed

is that he's not a stranger now

Table of Contents

A Collection of Strangers.............................1

Assorted Sentimentality..............................41

Regarding Love......................................87

A Collection of Strangers

A STRANGER ON A PLANE

I told my current woes to a stranger on a plane
I didn't even care if she saw me as insane
she told me hers too, and it made her cry
but dignity is secondary when you're in the sky.

At 30,000 feet the facade cannot survive
it plunges back to earth in a most tempestuous dive
we strangers left naked with what's real
without your pride it's so much easier to feel.

I'll admit sometimes I've put myself in danger
it's riskier when on the ground confiding in a stranger;
in coffee shops, on the clock, or in a written word
humanity seeks to hear and begs itself be heard.

In flight solitude you ought to count a loss;
a wasted chance to speak to those you never will recross
conversely, brief companionship may prove a gain
I, for one, live indebted to a stranger on a plane.

ADAM

Seven o'clock came an hour and a half late
but he was there a day early.

Epiphany:
I must have lost touch
fleeing the moment my servitude is complete
while he lingers.

Expensive jeans,
button up shirt,
gelled hair,
eyes seeking camaraderie
through the horn rimmed windows.

After dinner,
conversation for dessert

I'm being paid to talk to him
while he's doing it at cost
reminding me of a rich socialite
who mistakenly fell asleep in the taxi
and woke up
a waiter and a patron.

Suddenly I'm ashamed
I only put on a rushed coat of mascara
while we were his night on the town.

I'd forgotten what it's like to be lonely
how it makes confidantes
out of coworkers.

BETH

I met a love of my life (in a platonic way)
and I swear things are different now.

I gush
about how we would be best friends
if only she and I lived in the same state.

So brief was our acquaintence
like how at night
you can see for a moment
the world at its brightest
when the lightning flashes.

How she reminded me
of the feeling of sunshine
when the rain is over
while the smell of petrichor still hangs in the air.

What I will never understand
is why we limit love at first sight
to eros
as if a friendship is not worthy enough
to say

"When I saw you, I knew I loved you."

BILL

We built a castle where we reigned that day
on that cliff above the river bend
you and I, the highest of kings
that day you were my friend.

Your brother was a bore, you said
"Video games, to it there's no end!"
but we were rulers, he was common
so you became my friend.

I'd never met a kid named Bill before
but you your hand did lend
and never have I since known one
not since you were my friend.

For hours in the sand and sun we played
a day like that the years have yet to rend
Sarah Lynn was still a child back then
but you my better friend.

A lunchtime summons there rang out
a sovereign call, a mothersend
gone on peanut butter sabbatical
see you on the other side my friend.

Looking afterwards I never found you
so kings alone must fend
but you should know that on that day
you were my greatest friend.

CHESTER

Chester in the produce section walks
slow
too old for love
too young to not want it.

The grapefruits keep
    rolling
        down
while Earnie
and all the others who aren't Santa
garner looks from the children
who don't realize
they're looking at
just a group
of sad,
old men.

"Are the pomegranates good?"

Ma'am this is a Walmart
who cares?

Chester does.

They're decent
but nothing great
so she buys three.

Fumbling to open the plastic bag
she thanks him
and walks away.

Chester is still only an hour into his shift
he smiles,
love in his heart and a drag in his step
but no intention
of abandoning his post.

DAVID

He was an artist few people ever heard of
ending every note he sent with
"LOVE".

You're never going to see
his name in lights
but behind the stage he fit the part
as if it were a glove.

For a moment
the universe he directed
though his vision
none ever perfected
he thought we were golden
and by him never
was I rejected.

A grand and fleeting moment
he had to shine
and we all shared it
so it was also
mine.

But times like that never last
and in the end
I suppose that's fine.

DON & SHIRLEY

Two diet Cokes
endless refills of conversation
on nights so very different
from ones I don't like talking about.

When I think of them
I remember
all over again
the sudden discovery
of my belly content
vacant
of the complacent hunger
which gnawed at my laugh
and startled me awake
with the imagined sound of a Cisco ringtone.

A hearty thank you
to two kind souls
who reintroduced me to wakefulness
and simple
honest conversation.

My favorite times
when the snow would settle in
and in between the flurries
I espied headlights
at once rushing to ready the table
for the patrons who tipped me
generously
in kindness.

Telling jokes,
thawing my sense of humor,
never once casting doubt
on my declarations
of long distance love,
but instead offering stories and tales
the morals of which went something like
"*It often works out pretty well in the end.*"

Reminding me that changing the world
can look like two people
well past their youth
sitting down at a table
greeting their waitress
not knowing
the difference they are making
yet making it anyway.

ELI

I just found out that sweet young man
didn't have an accident.

The notion was there clawing at the back of my skull
but anyone can have a car accident
I must not allow myself to see suicide
in every darkened eye
or behind every shy veneer
but this time
it was there.

Now he is in the hospital
with a broken back
or neck —
I can't remember which
because when the car wreck left him alive
he sought a tall building.

Why do such good people
see the world and think
"This would be better if I were gone"?

I am glad he failed
because my best friend succeeded
and I can assure you

It is not better.

EVAN

Beware of poet boys and the pictures that they take
before they fall in love it's their own hearts they break.

A glass that's raised at twelve and all the city's light
this pack of lonely comrades won't scare away the night.

He always was a dreamer, I suppose, but in a darkened way
his heart it never laughed nor kept the woe at bay.

The strongest men are yet made weak by a pretty face
and they both fell, I saw it happen, but not selfsame pace.

A month or so then passed, and oh, too deep they delved
his pride became a beast and then their love was shelved.

Who knows if he was right, perhaps he may have been
but it was not his place to speak, and so he could not win.

Twixt madness and persistence the line is thinly drawn
and trotting down this path too far, how soon you will be gone.

A man once held a weight until with flesh it grew
he then forgot the freedom that once he **truly** knew.

To love against the odds, so noble we are told
but sometimes to let go is so much more than bold.

The sun will rise again at dawn and all into the day
but those who hide their faces soon see in only grey.

The lover and his hopeless love, he says that she's the one
but every day he ventures down to never greet the sun.

Melancholy is a faithful friend and if allowed won't leave
for selfishly he says
"It's only us, and I to you will cleave."

The girl the dreamer **loved** was full of light and dusk
and now the boy that once she knew becomes a ruined husk.

Every day he's less of who she loved and yet **he** cannot tell
the fastest cars are still too slow, the highest roof still hell.

People praise those with souls that they call old
but all that's left of him is bitterness and cold.

The most crowded club with the loudest noise, and still he is alone
Love's turned to cancer, yet he's proud of how it's grown.

One day perhaps he'll look **again** despising this his fate
but he's the one who chose it

and what if it's too late?

FLOYD

"I have one-thousand in my backyard!"

Having also had a good deal of wine
jubilant as could be
a gift of a ripe watermelon.

"Do you really?"
the lady asked.

Laughing,
the fat old man took his seat at the table.

*"If I had one-thousand I would have
gone to Europe to celebrate instead."*

Ordered his food
as a well worn song played out the
ambience of the scene.

And I thought to myself

what a wonderful world.

GEOFF

Flying on the trampoline
the smell of cut grass
a summer day utterly spent.

Small thin boy
falling out of breath
landing knees all bent.
The girl
already down
sits laughing.

Then a risky silence
followed by
Confession.
Suddenly,
the leaves are brown
woken up at thirty-five.

The falling still in his stomach
only now it feels like hunger.
He understands now
her lack of answer
was one
what he missed when he was younger.

Why she fled into the house
left him deserted in the yard
misplaced all her words.
His open heart exposed
his chance lost
it would seem.

Though it's probably too late
the man still smiled
as he relayed his dream.

HENRY

The artist in your heart
will find his way to your tongue.

Do not allow him
to get lost along the way
drowned by the others—
your brother.

You wanted me to be in love with him
but I could not bear
his taunting vendetta
wanting the artist in you dead.

I could not
be with one
who had symphonies in his hands
while using them to strangle
the simple tune
in yours.

IRIS

Whistling
in the card aisle
just browsing
for while
among the Valentines.

All of five two
her eyes
I think
were blue.

With glasses
and
light blond hair
such a crowded
bustling store.

I wonder who
she's whistling for
and if he whistles too.

JACK

He got off the school bus
loose jeans
over spindly legs
his shirt
tucked into his Levi's.

Picked up a nickel
just his luck
Jefferson would rather
face the blacktop
than some gawkish
high schooler.

Heavy brown work boots,
because surviving adolescence
in public school
is quite a job
when you've got
reliable and laborious aspirations.

The kind of person
who is no boy
the very definition of
a young man
but it's the young part
that sticks out
so comedically to others
like the Adam's apple
protruding from his
pubescent throat.

An open invitation to mockery
taking yourself seriously.

But when I saw him
I didn't laugh
because my former self
was once enamored
with a young man just like him.

And though we never met
I should like to think
we were old friends
but all he knows
is that he's
a nickel richer.

JOHNNY

The way the city looked that night
from out across the water
was enough to make this tourist ache.

That was when I still childishly thought
I might live there one day
sometimes I still think about it
for my own sake.

Painting the whole episode
with the colors of unrealistic expectations
and misplaced romantic perception
never mind the island is a dump
and getting off the boat
you'll find no friendly reception.

More often
I think about the man playing guitar
on the ferry
and how nobody listening
didn't stop him
from doing something scary.

I witnessed an artist
oozing with tired determination
wanting to make music
that will be remembered
past the day he'll die.

And to borrow a line from Billy Joel

***Between you and me
and the Staten Island Ferry
so do I.***

KRISTA

Nothing special about Starbucks.

Teenagers come from school
slurping their lattes
shot of espresso because the teachers suck
word in the locker room is
so did that girl.

Moms and construction workers
ordering to go
you know,
I never saw an employee there
who didn't have scars
"*Will you be having an identity crisis with the frap?*"

A wretchedly ordinary place
the mediocre song that's playing
every time you turn on the radio
except
in the corner
was a Parisian café
twinkle lights along German streets
friendly chatter from the balconies of Amsterdam.

The closest I've ever been to that boat
where Audrey and Cary kissed
a thirst for a town you've never been
cheap coffee won't quench it
but this is Tuscany wine.

Krista brought the world with her
if you could make out the photographs
through the blurry German accent.

Carried all her postcards with her
to remind herself the story is actually true.

Suddenly,
instead of coffee
rich brown beer.

Instead of music
the sound of soldiers dancing.

Instead of gossip
saccharine words from sweaty men.

This boozy respite from the late aftermath of war.

She had seen nearly the whole world
so why be stranded here?
even her hair seemed anxious to travel
by the way its frizzy curls leapt in all directions.

It felt a little like tragedy to me
to have felt the wind
in such romantic places
and settled for an air conditioner
in Statesville.

A hefty price
to pay for a dance
but probably
because
I never got to meet
the American
who took her home.

LUDA

The smell of fresh cut roses
while the gap of distance closes
in a hug that makes the bad less strong.

She asks how you are
and says

"You look beautiful."

Sweet Russian Tea girl,
I wished her arms from me would never unfurl.

She held you in a way
that held your tears at bay
because in her embrace
you realized how tired you were.

For the brief moment it was all on her.

And always,
always the roses.

LUKE

An artist of ink
what do you think?

He'll go places!

The look in his eyes
is not a disguise
the lovely lonely.

The blood from his pen
and the colors of when
days ran together.

Feeling the stings
remembering things
even if they happened
to someone else.

What I know to be true
just like when I first saw you
someone will look at him and think
"He's the most beautiful person I've ever seen."

MS. LOUISE

So many Sundays
back when I was a kid
I felt like an intruder
although my eyes I hid.

Crying, sobbing, pleading
the ancient lady in the second row
my dad would go sit with her
speaking soft and slow.

Guilt-ridden, scared, and old
Forgiveness she had had for years
but still in shame
she carried all her fears.

What sin had she done
that still burnt her with its embers?
I could make a guess
but not even God remembers.

MATTHEW

I didn't really want to dance with him.

He had asked me to be his date
a few weeks prior
my response:
I would share a dance
but not a date.

Not with anyone.

(*Meanwhile the back of my mind begged
the boy across the room to ask,
but by divine grace he never did.*)

The evening came
we didn't even speak
then I asked for the dance
I didn't really want.

Until I saw him smile
finally understanding
that he was
not rejected
but a true friend.

We swayed to *Wagon Wheel*
both thanked the other for the dance.

That was the last time we spoke
but I hear he's doing well.

NIGEL

The grey sidewalks in the biting bitter cold
cause most to lose their grace
as the layers 'round them fold.

All they need is February 14th
to remind them of their state
but then
walking towards me next the busy street
an orchid in his arms
a step-dance on his feet.

Our gazes aligned
and I knew it was love
by the marked purpose in his gait
the way his eyes squinted in a giddy style
in his own shoes glad for every mile.

Like two grave robbers
passing each other
on the way out of the cemetery
our gazes conjoined
we smiled
both happy for what the other had purloined.

OLIVER

I've never seen a gym rat
working at Starbucks
but there he is.

He is looking remarkably
mentally well
for a barista.

Come to think of it,
so are the others here too
I'm used to Starbucks employees'
having a tragic look about them
and scars up to their elbows.

I know he's a stranger
but it feels good
to see him like this
as if all baristas are the same person
and I am seeing
a friend recovered from a dark place.

PHOTO MAN

I wanted romance like the birds
whose dancing feet
will not be stilled
and whose parted feathers exposed
may find
their fragile hearts broken
when the invisible music
stops.

Foolishly
I pondered love
considered so many
but they never danced for me.

I have thrown them all away
but I keep in an honored place
of thanks
the ones who saved me
from what I have so often seen:
people settling
like pulp at the bottom of the glass.

Not I!

Dear handsome photo man
In the midst of grandeur
so lovely
something inside me was flying.

He was the reason I kept
the sunflowers.

It was unmistakeable
the look of dreams in his face
his long blonde hair tied back
a painting of soft thunder
living
every one of the moments
he spent his hours to capture.

The two sentences he spoke to me
and the brief eye contact

KA-THUMP!
Several notions off the refrigerator door
and into the trash.

I don't mind that I never saw him again
he made the difference
that was his to make.

I am so grateful for him
as the most beautiful man in the world
dances for me
and also likes the way I look
in sunflowers.

SARAH

Transfixed on the floor in front of the couch
while the boys played ping pong.

If I moved it might end
this affection from someone
not even a friend.

Four years old
and her in high school
I don't remember any of the others
but Sarah with her curled
blonde hair
and kind voice.

Her gentle hands
changed me very little
but nonetheless
forever.

I bet she made a good mother
she is the reason
I do it to others
because in a world
that so often doesn't care
I'd never felt so tangibly loved
as when she played with my hair.

SUMMER

The first time I met her
she made me afraid.

Though it shames me
I felt she was a bomb.

The nerve she had
to share my name.

The things written
in her face — I saw that she was bad.

But, although I was too old
for this sort of mistake
the next time
I saw
I had misread her face.

It did not say
"*bad*"
as I was so sure it did.

Instead I saw plainly
beneath her eyes
the word writ there was
"*sad*".

And I was grieved
for though I call myself an artist
I'd drawn a wrong conclusion.

So when I again decided
to aim to love her
I found I didn't have to
try anymore
because
I already did.

TAYLOR

To be perfectly honest
I sometimes forget he isn't related.

In the filing cabinet of my mind under
"*Brothers*"
there are three
and only when I examine very closely
do I see that one is not quite like the others.

I refuse to change it
because I've learned,
while it may not be factual
it has most definitely been earned.

With its chipped edges
the coffee table reminds me
like a moral in a fable
that before I was my husband's wife
they shared this house
teaching each other how to be good men
deciding what to make of life
occasionally putting thoughts to pen.

With every bottle cap I sweep out from under the couch
I see he is
to my lover
what I could never be.

So do not think it odd
that hearing the one I love most
say
"*I love you*"
to another on the phone
makes me feel a sense of gratified joy
and unbearable fondness.

I think he ought to know how much he's missed,
because while I'm the one and only wife
he's on a different list.

TRISTAN

Young Brad Pitt boy
Brad Pitt before Troy boy
running down the street.

The urgency,
as if making a resurgence
he
had to get there in time.

A rented tuxedo slung over his shoulder
while the March winds blew colder
a different century
everyday sense of adventure
we
haven't seen in so long.

Hometown simple glory
I'll put you in a story
not mine
but one for
the
people who say you don't exist.

Like the layers in his hair
is the romance to those who
care
this kind not sexual
not sensual
but present tense
you'll
find it still struggles on.

I hope he made it in time
for unknown reason or
rhyme
and whatever else is true
I hope that one day
someone runs that way
for you.

ULYSSES

Is this what it's like to go to war?

Castmates being your brothers in arms
the stakes are much lower
but still worth the toil
because tonight
on this stage I would die for you
and behind it
we would cut our wrists
so that we might bleed a pact
written in disappearing ink.

For in six months
I won't even be able
to call you
my friend.

VICTORIA

I knew you by your smell as soon as you walked in.

At least this time it really is you
instead of a stranger
who also happens to wear
Warm and Cozy
by Victoria's Secret.

I can smell it from across a crowded room
pick it out among the other scents
like a diamond among broken glass.

The way it brings back
a specific era of my youth
and lovely,
tragic people
I don't know anymore.

WALLACE

So many people
the Empire State steeple
the dolorous and bedizen
those who need more "medicine"
like the man with yellow eyes,
the city lords and jettisoned.

On the subway
a multitude of kinds.

"Don't make eye contact!"
my mom said avoiding the attention
they wanted to attract.

What caught my eye
and got stuck in my heart
sitting across and apart
a rough cut man
I see him clear and plain
eating a muffin on the train.

Swiss army knife
cutting into bites
such intentionality
the like I'd never seen.

Such a simple grace
for such a rushing place
the greatest city in the world
where history unfurled
and I couldn't stop seeing
a man who wasn't busy
just being.

I said to myself
"I'll write about him one day"
because I so loved the way
he wasn't lonely
but I
being a procrastinator
waited four and a half years later
while he finished his muffin
and still got home on time.

YOU

In every room
on every sidewalk when the raindrops turn to steam
between the lines of every list of names
that comes across my desk
inside of every dream
I am looking for you.

Perhaps the way a drunk looks for his lost lover at the bottom of his glass
only to discover too late
that it's his own reflection
and his head is up his ass.

But I like to hope it's different
having felt it for strangers
and strangers who stopped being strangers
I am aways looking for another.

Is it wrong to want to expand my collection?
Because
while my father-in-law collects every unique root beer bottle
I'm collecting faces and names
people to be in love with, but not in a lover's way
That is reserved for one.

But the way I feel for you and the strangers in the city
The awful thing is
I sometimes forget them
and it's such a pity.

ZEB

I was looking for something on the beach
and he asked what it was
"I don't know, but I will when I find it."
I swore I felt it just out of reach.

Walk with me awhile
he did.

I asked him about his life
he told me
how a long time ago
he'd had a wife

I told him I was engaged
good thing you can still feel melancholy
when you're in love
the hurt I never want to assuage.

The man had been at war in 1973
the Yom Kippur in Israel
remembrance of it raised the hair on his arms
he showed me.

Making sandy footprints just out of waves' reach
he was what I was looking for
when I stepped out there
alone on the beach.

Silence
comfortable silence
and then a goodbye.

I returned to the house with a few shells
where I thought
how we
going two different ways
were for a moment parallels.

The man with the kind face,
tan skin,
bushy mustache
what I was looking for
among the seabirds' din.

The shells I gathered that day I no longer keep
but as for my companion on the beach
I walk with him
on nights when I cannot sleep.

Assorted Sentimentality

THE OPEN WINDOW

In the pale light
all alone I woke tomorrow
and creeping to the window pane
I saw the streaming sorrow.

It seemed as though I only viewed
the end of lines that blur
and burdened, carried the valise
of things which never were.

A page came tossed upon the wind
such things I saw thereon
a tale of things that might have been
ambitions long since gone.

Then staggering forth I caught the script
between my fingers cold
and read such words as never spoke
a tale that must be told.

My eyes did scan the parchment
until my heart bled raw
I read and found that non-existence
is the gravest flaw.

A child it spoke of
a girl who fell asleep one summer afternoon
the window open brought a dream
that stuffy day in June.

The boy she saw in sleeps' bright world
had brought with him two pails
with these they spent that sacred nap
in search of tiny snails.

When once she woke she felt alight
with friendship, though a dream
but sleeping with the window open
is more than it would seem.

As she grew her playmate stayed
growing at her pace
and when the window kept ajar
she'd meet his boyish face.

Then one day at sweet sixteen
they took an autumn jaunt
and when he kissed her virgin lips
he proved more than just a sleeping haunt.

For three long years the window never shut
but stayed—
It was his door to her,
and she was three years unafraid.

Until the day she came back home,
her heart a heavy weight
a man had asked her for her hand
and they had set the date.

He was a good man really
she never could deny
and to refuse his love
she found no reason why.

The two were wed
and she was none the worse
but never could the days with one
the other reimburse.

Then children came,
and she grew older every moment hence
until by chance the window cracked
in blessed negligence.

She fell to dreaming and he was there
just as he'd always been
so handsome and so beautiful
two lovers without sin.

He knew and loved her still
in spite of passing years
but only living in her dreams
a face behind her tears.

The world of wakefulness
and the one of sleep
to two her life belonged,
but both she could not keep.

A vigil in the sleeping world
this man ceased not to hold
"But of reality and dreams" she said
"the difference must be told!"

She longed to stay forever
loving him in every human way
but she knew the ties which bound her
in the coming of the day.

Her man of dreams stroked her hair
and her frame caressed
Her cries were muffled
and to her tears his damp shirt did attest.

The two communed together
their hopeless state lamented
and from the harshness of their plight
the noble hearts dissented.

She told him of her duty
to the world of brazen day
he sadly smiled for he had known
there was no other way.

She said goodbye to him,
the window must stay shut
and when he knowingly kissed her cheek
it was the deepest cut.

As the sun began to rise
he faded from her view
and with a shudder she dressed her child
to duty staying true.

The window closed for many years
as dust did settle thick
till she at four score and a month
in bed with age was sick.

The June was humid
even to the end of day
her hand in her husband's
now at ease did lay.

He had showed himself a faithful man,
and kind.
She couldn't see his wrinkled face
for her eyes at last were blind.

"You know I've always loved you, dear,"
he whispered in a rasp
*"even though your love
I could never fully grasp."*

She sighed and pressed his hand,
sorry for his loss to be
he said, "*I know you now will go to one
who's far more loved than me.*"

She now did realize
few men there are like this
and pausing asked a favor
bestowing then a kiss.

That the window be opened
as she forever fell asleep
so without a grudge he sowed this deed
from which he'd never reap.

As eternity dawned upon her
young again she seemed
and waiting there with arms outstretched,
the one of whom she'd dreamed.

CLEAVAGE

I was looking
through a collection
of neglected dreams
and other things
I found in the attic.

I took the rubble,
so tacky when
illuminated   ai
by the present   nt   n.
                                ou
into   the m
     the   of
          clea age
             v
She comforted them
between
her grassy slopes,
soothed them against
her windy breast.

Added to the many
embarrassments
that stick like rocks
in the hearts of people
who were young
until they stopped dreaming.

COLORADO

I was terrified of you
and your kind face
golden hair tumbling down your back
like a river of autumn aspen leaves
I was scared it was the noose
that was to strangle the oxygen from my dreams.

The embraces that I should have returned
so much more fervently
friendly words were like threats to me,
and the way he and I would laugh together in class
or when any of the handsome men
opened their eyes in my direction
while I willed the cells of my body
every trace of myself
to turn invisible.

The girls who I never became friends with
for fear they were you in disguise
I wonder if I miss them now.

The snow too,
an antagonist
the unwelcome thrill rushing through me
at every first, second, and thousandth sight of those infernal flakes.

Retreating to my wine colored sheets
intoxicating myself with sleep
to escape meeting you.

I never did
though so many times
I wondered if I had
slipping out the window
every time I heard your friendly feet at the door
stayed quiet lest you
would swiftly whisk me into a conversation
enrapturing me
with the way you built your paragraphs
fashioning traps out of jests
and nets from your eyelashes
discovering too late
you were never coming for me at all.

SUMMERTIME WHILE IT STILL HOLDS WONDER

Summertime comes like a lover.

She makes a bed of the grass
and imbues it with her verdant scent.

A beautiful dream
we've known her forever
yet didn't fall in love with her
until we were in our prime.

Embracing our bodies,
she leaves her breath
as mist on our foreheads
and calls us to lie under the stars.

She lets fall torrents of happy tears
and laughs at our drenched state.

Hold her as long as she allows
and savor her presence —
it will not last.

Autumn is a boon,
winter is a taskmaster,
and spring is a child.

Of all the seasons only summer is a bedmate.

When she leaves
you will miss her
windy fingers through your salty hair
but like a bad habit
you will drink her in all the more
the next time she returns.

SYMBIOSIS

You and he are always together lately
laughing. Talking. Confiding.
I watch because no one is here
talking to me.

A secondhand warmth I suppose
is better than none.

I trail along
the one who walks behind
when the sidewalk isn't wide enough for three.

I give you two a sense of legitimacy, of right
a proper third wheel.

This must be what it's like to date
except lonely.

I know I'm loved
you both tell me so while you stand
holding hands together.

I don't doubt it
even though I'm the one taking the picture
for the two of you
we'll get another one with all three of us you say
but we never do.

I'm not trying to abandon my station,
I have become a pro at this
it gives me hope
and the familiar ache of longing.

Symbiosis
Remember that word from biology?
A relationship where both benefit:
I'm the person keeping you from being alone,
together.

What a travesty that would be!
You both keep me from being alone,
alone.

I'm the guardian of propriety
I guess
but you're the one falling
while I'm the one getting motion sickness
because it's bittersweet
tagging along on someone else's adventure
but it's better than having
no adventure at all.

THE WEST

The reddest castles rise blooming just beyond
and tiny suns delight the way
the coarseness still is not unfeeling
the wild
undulating play.

The quiet man who reads his paper
but cannot keep the hands of his eyes
from touching his wife.

The dishes can wait
the red rocks say
come, let's roll in the grass
that with wildflowers is rife.

The pines heed the well worn passion
the mountains are so unsafe
his arms about her waist in a lover's fashion.

Would you have it any other way?
Would you tame their wild taste?
Would you ruin them with safety
and lay their secrets waste?

The consummation of the peaks with the sky
his fiery lips on hers
blended in a holy light
that bathes the stoic firs.

The roughest hands may have a loving touch
the western wind against a naked neck
and like a woman led to love
inhibitions this land will wreck.

NONSENSE

Where does it go?
Why does no one say?

The TV doesn't show where it all ends
or if children play in it
riding their tricycles around and around
until it gets dark
and the street lamps come on.

The air smells
like lightning bug juice
the breeze lets them feel
how quickly
they are growing up.

Then they run through the yards
everyone will come out again
tomorrow.

I think there are trees
dark, lush woods
why didn't I ever explore them?

The houses are warmly lit,
flower beds around the lampposts
maybe I only think it's like that
because that's how mine was
I guess I was too young to care
that there was a hill
with horses on it
at the end of the jungle.

Maybe it is nothing at all like that
just orange and white reflectors
on the guardrails
at the far end
of a deserted circle of asphalt
where it never rains
so rain's never late.

You can't go further
so just use it
the cul-de-sac at the end of the interstate.

CONSTITUTION

The window facing the terrace
is flung open
its curtains swaying
gracefully inward
as the morning sunlight flows through
spilling richly into the room
bringing with it
the fragile scent
of the oncoming spring
which seems as though it would vanish
into the cold lapse
of the presiding winter
were it inhaled but a little too heartily
for its dainty constitution.

A MOMENT FROM 2020

The happenings that be
a metamorphosis of cloud
into cotton candy
and Sprite
poured out pink
while cicadas sing
the summer
to death.

though it isn't yet august
they're just preparing
while we strum
into the dusk
always
dr i f t i n   g   .

THE END OF AN ERA

I cracked my phone screen
it had survived 4 years
under my
tolerable care.

Caseless
at 14,000 feet
photos in the snow
a whole summer
completely unprotected
but not the day after.

I guess it goes to show
a hero won't always
die like one.

Sometimes they just
fall on the porch
as they're coming in
from the battle.

THE FISHERMAN

Sitting
on his ramshackle boat
dipping
below the surface
the worm sways to the tune
while the milky way acoustics
turn the night
into an amphitheater.

Humming a made up melody

Good food, fine wine
Take this woman, make her mine.

The fish don't bite
and now
the worm
is waterlogged.

THE NIGHT FLIGHT

I was only six at the time
in the bedroom with the bunny wallpaper
but the sky that night sublime.

Feeling myself grow up made my heart ill
how long did I stand there
stars in my eyes, trapped behind the window sill?

My sister slept, and I cannot help but feel
she missed something big
and maybe something real.

Who can say if she would have felt it then
but it attached itself to me
still hanging about the words conceived by pen.

For the first time I saw
the blueness of the night
and ambling across the window some lonely nameless flight

The clouds like perfect crisscross stitching laid
as if God had for the sky
a pair of fishnets made.

I grieved there behind the glass
being sentenced to only spectate
the plane so freely pass.

The first time I ever felt that ache
which now is like a well worn pair of shoes
or a thirst that can't be slaked.

It hurt my throat to think of this
knowing all those passengers went somewhere together
and my unknown presence did not miss.

I have seen many nights
that even the angels would astound
but never has one so much as that made me loathe the ground.

GINGER CAT

The smell of change hangs in the air
feeling a loss over leaves
I was never acquainted with
just because
I am old friends with the trees they belonged to
while a dog I didn't grow up with
sits at my side.

Like the brown that has leaked
into the white of his eye
seconds cannot be penned
like beasts in a zoo
or words on a page
not the army of months which advanced on us
even while we lay dreaming in summer's bed.

So the pup takes in
the scent of melancholy
and afternoons you forgot to make note of
suddenly
feeling himself older than he used to be
lets fall a heavy sigh
while the ginger cat wails on
having felt it
such a long, long time.

BATH

Silver in the chlorophyll
while the trunks stand ironclad,
riches untouchable
lie diamonds on the grass.

Every inch of the exposed
feels 1,000 times more naked
bidding the concealed
come out and play.

The imperfect turned to angels
you could run forever
the sparkling blades
lending wings to your feet
while the earth makes way.

The harshness of the sun
like a thundering shower
ended none too soon
and if you turn off your light
you can take a bath in the moon.

CONTACTS

Sifting through contacts
compiled since age 11
porcelain figurines
arranged about the house
such intentionality by a madwoman
pacing about her echochamber of an inbox
occasionally taking inventory
of her glass-eyed friends
just to prove they still exist.

Hoarding them like hostages
they are unaware of their entrapment
and some have lost recognition
if they ever even had it
faces worn smooth and featureless,
colors faded to sickly yellow
but still they remain.

Some freshly dusted
though
they'll never be what they once were
when they were made for late night
cameraderie
and ingenuous
Flirtations.

Others are kept
in the attic
with the webs
and read receipts.

If only they could be restored,
but the steps to the attic
are splintered
and unsteady
creaking
beneath a layer of dust
and things that ought not
have been sent.

Some get thrown out
while others are taken out

and contemplated —
even admired
from time to time
before being returned
to their tissue paper wrappings
saved for a time when something can be found
to break the long, long silence.

PASSING

The day came in on the usual train
technical nitpickers will say it arrived at midnight
people who live the day know 12 AM
is still last night.

But anyway
when it stepped onto the platform
into the footprints of all that had preceded
it was the same shoe size
of 24 hours.

Its face so familiar
one could have easily mistaken it for
any of the others.

I suppose it took a reasonable number of lives
while seeing the start of others.

I barely spoke to it
until it was nearing its departure
I was unexpectedly smitten
an embrace that left my face red
and my neck sweaty.

Its kiss
was the summertime
I wished it not to go
seeing it tip its hat
and board the train
I noticed my finger bleeding.

You might laugh
but I kept the green bandage
while my friend kept a scar.

PROM - A FEVER DREAM

Loud thumping rhythms
assaulting conversation
pounding on the door to our minds
"Let me into your feet so you can dance!"
when all we really wanted
was to feel comfortable.

The shining dresses
swirling
synthetic fog
and lights like the London blitz
the smell of warm fabric and sweat.

Cologne
It either makes you want
or want to want
the reason some of the girls
put their bodies
against a near stranger
but in the end
they wake up feeling foolish
and the number never gets called.

WAVE

You know those places in the road
where the speed limit is high,
abreast the road the trees are nigh,
and curves sneak up before you've slowed.

You beg God not to meet another
going the opposite way
of all the things to pray
we met against my druthers.

It's the fear is of derailment
a collision to be clear
I met you there, wishing I was here
your companionship an ailment.

From that danger I am saved
the road henceforth is straight
I was anxious until it was too late
I now regret I never waved.

FRIENDS?

A message to the friends I don't see anymore:
I cannot say that you never leave my mind
for many days go by
between my thoughts of you
but this much is true:

The moments you grace my memory
or enter my internal dialogue
and the way
when I hear a joke you would think funny
I laugh for the both of us
I take to mean that our friendship isn't dead.

It just thrives less in real life
than it does in my head.

THE CONSCIENCE-MAN

We walked along the rubbish trail
just below the sky
through silty graves of yesterdays
went the Conscience-man and I.

A clammy vice grip on my hand
my lukewarm beating breast
the stench of all uncovered tombs
for the hoarded dead no rest.

Galloping on to far worse things
my macabre companion grinned
even the good it seemed
was just the rot re-skinned.

The fish-headed scents that stalked
intestines congealed in a jelly bowl
the erotic call of demented sights
sinew-flossed leers haunting every hole.

He showed me the hideous sights
wrought from my own hands
stretching past acceptable plains
'twas I despoiled these lands.

Banished to my self-made hell
squalor, my food, drink, and breath
deserving it by far the worst
I hoped to meet my death.

A stranger then ahead was seen
my eyes, could they be flayed?
I looked to my companion
but he seemed unafraid.

Neither friends nor enemies
a handshake and a knowing glance
at once my hand was freed
they both retained their stance
observed my gaping need.
I chose to love the stranger,
though he had loved me first
then saw the putrid filth was vanished
the ground was made un-cursed.

"Thank you for your time," I said.

He bowed,
"To others I must fly.
I always meant to bring you here."
Then parted ways
the Conscience-man and I.

AIRPORT TENSION

Threads like spider webs
the tension hanging like a dewdrop in the morning time
after a hundred nights with no unusual action
brushes by in a whorl of esoteric thrills previously unknown
except in vicarious fictions of the mind.

The exotic waft of sleeplessness and cologne
upon making the laborious ascent up the whirring escalator
and as the altitude increases so does the unfounded desire
to commit both violence and an act of passion—
a furious kiss between two strangers
the contents of whose luggage will never even meet
or to challenge to a duel for the mere prospect
of having the nerve to be neighbors in age.

The loudspeaker crackling its tenuous gossip
begs to see the finality of this unspoken dance
both parties conscious of which partners
they have taken without permission
while they wordlessly spar in air so thick
not a word can pass between them.

Glances are daggers and every blink is very provocative
even better when they are forced to occupy adjacent seats—
angel-people to wrestle with
until heaven is out of sight again
or to embrace as the ground charges upwards like an army
set to expunge the bird from its horizon.

VISITATION

Who knocks at this
the witching hour?

The poor luck to be awake
at such a haunted time.

Knocking, knocking on the door
if perchance the knocker were sleep
prudence would let him in
but sleep does not pound like that.

Dare to don slippers and a robe
to push back the curtains
create a sliver of sight.

Please, let the knocker be sleep
in this
the witching hour.

Oh dear!
Now you've seen its face!
Sleep will not visit at all tonight.

Who is it?
You know it well
it's that embarrassment from awhile back
and he has made well sure
sleep tonight is barred from this door.

BONES

When I was a kid
I made a fatal mistake that
in so many ways
almost didn't happen
but it did.
Since then I've kept it hid
but it didn't go away
even when the years piled up on top
I'd get close to it — then stop
not able to surmount the barrier
my subconscious built around it.

Until I stood at the wall
at the grave
looked at myself and forgave.

My pen was my shovel
and the memories scurried
but I dug and at last I unburied.

So there it was,
just as on the day it was done
and the following week
and every time I went to secretly seek
there with the shamefulness
of how much it hurt
when the blue had turned dull by the dirt.

But I saw it for what it was at last
a failure, a tragedy that happened too fast
but it wasn't so awful as it seemed.

And I'll dig it up as many times as I must
over and over till my ink turns to rust
letting it decompose beneath the stones
until one day I find it's only bones.

HATS ON OUR WALL

They watch us every single night and day
without a word of commentary yet.

They must have gathered their own opinions
and it's known that hats do not forget!

The cotton fields where they came from
or sheep from which they were shorn
never had such a close and personal view
if they had, I shouldn't think they'd scorn.

The bucket hats,
I think
love the comedy.

The honeymoon hat,
late talks
and tears.

The baseball caps are voyeuristic peeping Toms—
how dirty!

The adventure hats love
when we face our fears.

Though hats we know cannot forget
they have yet to disclose what's been seen
I suppose our secrets wear safe with them,
and once put through the wash will come out clean.

PRIDE

Treacherous inquiries and boastings
like the tragic opportunist
crying out into the night
"Absalom, oh to seize the heart's desire!"
while the lovers dream to set sail
their fingers in the black river
of spice-anointed curls
trickling down their strands
to a private audience with utter destruction.

When all the king's horses and all the king's men
unfurl their ranks in pursuit
not at all timorously does he fly.

Do you fear more
the man
or what brought his end?

For the only thing God had to do
was see that the tree had been planted
in due time.

ALASKA

Raw air and oatmeal for breakfast
a cup of darkness to go
tramping out into the stale snow.

Would you believe I can smell the fish
and feel their internal wetness?

Bits of flesh and scattered scales
on my freezing hands and wrists.

The bleakness is like a drug
for the happily unhappy.

An addict of a dope I've never had
but I would find it in the belly
of a thousand gutted fishes
and in the bottom of my whiskey glass
while we talked through the endless night.

But I know
as soon as the hot shower touched my skin
I would hate the name Alaska
until the next morning
when my fix would crash into my lungs
riding on the back of every wave
charging
like a moose
whose lost its young
thrilled to have cause for violence.

THE IDIOT

Perched by the lamp
foot half uncovered on the table
chipped by opening evening bottles of beer.

Accidentally beautiful,
statuesque, delicate.

Teetering on the fringe of a tragedy
that wasn't allowed to happen
and is now well passed.

The book, holding its breath
a comma.

The leaves quivering
under eyes
finally
reading the story
It has been telling
the adjacent pages
for God knows how long.

The inward tremble
upon finally
being touched.

Not moving
lest it might be closed
acting its own title
The Idiot.

CONFIDENTIALLY...

When someone
beautiful
and wild
tells you
something intimate
there is a rush
the hiss
of compressed air
escaping the bottle
of a drink
too strong
for most lips.

THUNDERSTORM

Even a thunderstorm
has its vulnerable moments
the brief instant you confided in me
like when the wind blows
exposing the underside of the leaves
right before the crash
and the invincible downpour.

I can still see the stain on your sleeve
even after your heart
has been safely hidden once again
the house inside obscured
by an impenetrable army of rain.

GROUNDHOG

Become infatuated
with the sight
of groundhogs
those little gentlemen
monitoring
the goings and comings
like little worker men
or dads peering out their windows
when someone turns around in the driveway.

PRESENT

Waterfalls shrouded
by a silver mist
and skies
with pink clouds kissed.

We think
the most beautiful places
are the ones we haven't been
our favorite people
the ones we haven't seen.

Perhaps
but what about
the field across the road
glistening
the morning after being mowed.

Or how
a hundred pumpkin plants
where it had been bare
planted by the pigs
who snooze the days out there.

I agree,
there are many places
I have dreams to see
but while I dream I mustn't miss
what's right in front of me.

NOOSE

I wish I could have told her
why I was sad.

Alas, they are my griefs
but not my secrets
It's the right to confide I wish I had
but I will not suffer
my lips to be loose
for weighty words
set free too soon
will prove to be a noose.

TOAD

If you shut me out one day
and refused to let me back in
I couldn't bear to stay away
so I'd live my life alongside yours
a whisper in the din.

Then when you forgot to guard
like a sleeper on the road
however badly you were scarred
I'd bring you my heart
the way a cat brings home a toad.

FRIENDS

Remember how
when we were kids
you leaned over
during the opening credits
of Napoleon Dynamite
and said,
"This song is how it was when we met."

How we could tell
we were gonna be friends.

Now looking back
knowing how it ends
I wish I could have taken you back there, see,
only I would have said it this time
to let you know
you always had a friend in me.

DUST TO DUST

The rain
will pack
the old dirt down.

There is no such thing
as fresh soil
however many
years they toil.

The wise man said
"There is nothing new under the sun"
and now
he is old dirt too
just like
everyone
he knew.

COURAGE

Courage
the wisp
of fleeting smoke
when inhaled
pumps the blood
faster than the words
can detonate
"Could I get your number?"

A moment later
and the ask
would have been drowned
by the dryness
in your throat.

But whatever
the fears were,
as the digits
are neatly folded
and put away
like warm laundry
you realize
they never
could have been
any others.

Regarding Love

THE BEGINNING

Who knows what will happen?
I was so unprepared
and yet it was perfect
so I let you hold me
till five.

So passed
the summer
now the aspens
are turning gold
the evening air
smells like vanilla
as the sun dips
below the peaks
that will soon
be covered in snow.

You send me the pages
onto which your thoughts spill
and I wonder,
how are you
so beautiful?

I met the man of my dreams
And it turned out
we were old strangers.

It scares me sometimes —
I drive myself half mad
all the books on your shelf
never told how this story ends
or whether your cat
ever comes to love me.

JULY

Walking to my bed
wondering if I'm already asleep
gravel on my naked feet
the stars like a billion
magnificent uncertainties
am I messing up?

"Trust me."

It's past midnight in Paris
and my hand still isn't sure
if it was really holding his.

Should I stop this now?

"Trust me."

HISTORY

I had a dream that I missed you
and upon waking
found nothing had changed.

Sometimes I can almost feel
your arm about my waist
but I don't have to look
to know it isn't there.

When you use my name
preceding those three most potent words
there's a pang in my heart
and it shows on my face
but you're not here to see it.

The first time you said you were in love with me
was the happiest moment of my life
and history repeats itself
a hundred thousand times.

HOW I MISS YOU

I didn't think you'd changed at all
you were just as I'd supposed you'd be
so why did I feel something like surprise
when you smiled
and looked that way at me.

Distance has some mysterious amnesic effect
its ill conceived attempt to soften
the blows of missing you
but it's nothing to regret, you know
It means I'll be taken once again when discovering what I already knew.

You're still so far away, now, and for awhile
the you that lives in my mind grows dim
Oh well, he's never been around
I still love that man, but you well over him.

It'll be better soon and I this ache will lose
seeing you
and feeling too will ease the strain
vanquishing the cold.

THE HEAVY DISTANCE

I thought one day I'd cry
because I drove so many places
without you
singing for the same reason
a cat purrs when it's cold
waking to days I knew
would not find me
looking you in the face.

I felt your absence so keenly
only described it to those who wouldn't worry:
myself and God
after all, we already knew about it.

A few strangers listened too
I fought with myself over you
you need never hear those fears
that took up space in my mind
and gave me depths
from which I wrote.

I penned a lot of letters I didn't mail
a lengthy poem had closure
so I tore it up.

Like a throbbing headache behind my ribs
in a solid mass
I remember everything I felt
heavy like a mountain
that I brought home
but our warmth had melted the snow
so it was lighter.

Sure one day
a cathartic avalanche would begin
becoming water
tears,
eroding the rock
sobs,
like an earthquake
shaking,
nothing but rubble.

Maybe one day it will happen
in one cry, the mountain gone
I've yet to sob
Sniffles and whimpers
with watery eyes
is all that's come;
Because what's bringing down the mountain
boulders to rocks,
pebbles to powder,
is this:
Instead of weeping
I've laughed.

WORRIES OF A LOVE

You should really just grab me 'round the waist and kiss me!
I think that would be apropos
much better than my going to the mailbox
coming back with a sappy smile
and a tan envelope among the bills.

I know you are in love with me
you tell me the good and the bad
and I don't hide anything from you
that I'm not hiding from myself.

I am determined to be more honest with you
tell you the things that I think about:
the lovely little things that matter to me
the things that worry me
— see, I ordered that last line after the first
because I didn't want it to seem like a big deal.

SHOULDERS

A waterfall cascading over angled rocks
worn smooth
by the mountain water
the booming of sublime
tingling coldness
assails your skin
with drops
of liquid thunder
unable to see the cliff
absorbed by its suggestion
the seismic swell
that rises with the water
on its
      long
        and
          unrestrained
           tumble
            over
           the
           crags
a quarry of ardent insinuation
the booming
of profound reverent violence
pulchritude only made evident
by boulders that mold the fall.

The shape of your shoulders
through your shirt:
one of the greatest things
I've ever seen.

AS COOKING IS TO SEX

If you would just stand there
doting over me
while I hide the fact
the knife
briefly mistook my finger
for a potato.

Wait for me to stop
pretending I know what I'm doing
as I season the food,
your hands around my waist
the oven temperature
slowly

```
            g.
         n
       i
     s
   i
 r
```

I think making love
is a lot like cooking sometimes
even though I
only
have cooking experience.

Some instinct tells me
there's something
the two share
both fill a human need
sealing the heart
with a caulk
that is
love.

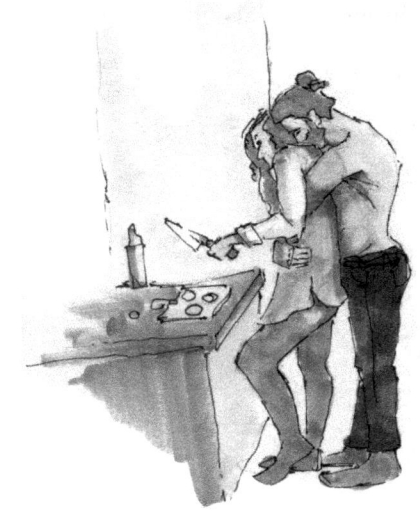

WANTING

You are the ocean to me.

My greatest desire
to drown myself
and lie saturated in the belly of the sea.

The currents which once tossed and pulled,
the wanting,
endless, turbulent wanting
now satisfied lies culled.

The waves that chopped into a foamy brine
with the hungry passion
of a tide I called mine
now swell and subside
like the rhythm of the music
we make with our hips.

The thirst that plagued and racked my frame
is quenched by your lips
replaced with your name.

MY COWS

Combing out the tangles of the land
is better when you're holding someone's hand
so I'm glad you can drive with only one
'cause sitting with you I know where I stand.

I must have fallen prey to a bit of casual sleep
so failing with you to vigilance keep
you stay steady so on you I'm counting
counting cows instead of sheep.

YOU'VE GOT MAIL

It was the happiest moment of my life
the distance like an inner gash
but I embraced this respite from the knife.

Meg Ryan and Tom Hanks writing to each other
while we were finally able to let fall our pens
and through locked lips the worries for a while smother.

Then a pause
you said
"Do you realize I'm completely in love with you?"
I said
"I know."

And that was it:
the happiest moment of my life.

How the following months
I was still afraid we would end sadly
because in the words of the film
"I wanted it to be you. I wanted it to be you so badly."

IMPORTANT

Things that are too important to be seen:
the inside of a sunset
the beginning of a dream.

What does the internal shift look like
when the like turns into love?
and the moment you discover
it's nothing like you dreamed of?

Where yesterday came from,
and where today goes
how did this all happen?
Nobody knows.

Some things are too important to be seen by us
some too important to be seen by anyone else.

One thing you have shown me is this:
It's really, very important
when we kiss.

I DON'T NEED THE MOON, JUST YOU

What if our dreams stay just that
and when Mowgli dies we just get another cat?

Would you think you had failed
if you published well writ books
but never put to sea?

Would you feel trapped living life with me?

On the porch with the kids
while the crickets sing their song
would you feel like that was wrong?

like maybe somewhere else is where you really belong?

I don't want you to regret
or miss what you will get
we have more ideas than years to live them.

You tell me I'm enough
I know you aren't one to bluff
I hope you're satisfied with me as I am with you.

If ever you're hit by some lying notion
don't ever start to doubt my unwavering devotion.

Like another man who wanted to sail the ocean
but did more important things
You're the greatest man in the world to your wife
and I want you to love this wonderful,
wonderful life.

MORNINGS

It's a funny,
funny thing to kiss
when you aim but then you miss.

Lips on teeth should not delight me
but when I hear you laughing
and feel your shaking frame
how my chest leaps when then I say your name
a charge like lightning in my veins.

Because I'm your Christmas-headed wife
who isn't going anywhere
not unless you've led me there.

All the others I've seen,
to them you're incomparable
with your book,
your thoughts,
and your sweater
till I take the place on your lap.

No urgent facts to build a conversation
so we'll sit here until we make some
love
to give the kisses you cannot return.

To make you laugh is more than I could earn
those wrinkles when you smile
I'll make them so much deeper.

Of this happiness I can't tell if I'm the sower or the reaper.

BESIDE

Brevity and permanence
how they go so fast down here
but it's still the first night
high up in the firmament.
The way the leaves catch hold of each other
as they drift on down the stream
and then again are parted
far sooner than would seem.

There's some I thought the current
would keep me close in stride
but now I look around
and it's only you beside.

POETRY

It feels like we are lovers in a book that's bound in leather
with cloth-like pages
by constant reading weathered.

The best parts over and over,
like the morning on the bridge
a realization that in the throat caught her
when the sun made lines beneath the water
wondered if she'd have lines like that
after he put a baby inside her.

A happy kind of melancholy
silence thin and holy
when even a breath sounds like thunder.

An unrushed readiness
toward the things that are to come
contentedness is anything but numb.

Then he finishes his pipe
and kisses her
not stopping
until she's shared a good deal of the smoke.

So heavy and profound, the weight of being one
even the rails on the bridge bend
as if it weighed a ton.

"It all sounds like poetry."
says the poet.

"What does?"

"Well everything, right now."

She's so glad to
see him know it.

THE SAME THINGS ARE THE BEST THINGS

My favorite writer
shares a bed with me.

Even with his straightforward way of thinking
he seems not to tire of the way
I say the same things
every time
I see him with his glasses on
or when he asks me how I am
or when we make love.

And when I fail to describe the dream I had
he still listens
pulling me onto his lap,
tucking my hair behind my ear with his fingers.

And when he's written all his books
I'll be the only one I know
who makes their favorite author laugh.

JUMPING TO CONCLUSIONS

My dad once told me
just how little he could see
when a girl wrote him letters
after he went away.

But when you said you'd write
I saw us married all right.

All the others aside
this one was no illusion
the best conclusion I ever jumped to
was ending up with you.

I FORGET

I used to say I never wanted to forget anything,
even the things that stuck in my gut
The dull and throbbing stings
doors that won't stay shut.

I valued the friendly harassments
that hurt for the way they were true
oh, the melancholic days that I spent
and the wistfulness I could accrue.

I pondered every friend I had lost,
wondered if the dues had been paid
what it had cost
when our time to rest had been laid.

Now it's all different
now I know you
my thoughts have been bent
some kinds dwindle to few.

I'm forgetting so much that I used to know
things no longer fit that I used to say
nothing about me resembles a show
and nothing has ever been so okay.

How to feel lonely I do not remember
or even how to hide
what it's like to live in December
but only on the inside.

Of all the things that up and took a hike
one woke so many joys anew
the way that I forget what it's like
to not be loved by you.

TUCKED IN

Some things are so pure
there isn't any cure
for their lack in a life.

It feels wrong to talk about them
as if from goodness shame could stem
but who wants to be seen like that?

Funny how getting caught
is suddenly fraught
when it's something simple and kind.

Receiving it is harder to face
once it starts taking up space
and time in your mind.

It feels like a risk to admit
it mattered when you decided to sit
and play with my hair.

How when you tucked me in
I took a nap with a grin
Though I was miserably ill
I'm reliving it still.

BUTTCHEEK

Sleepy words on dusty pages
in the early morn
thinking softly through last nights scenes
finding such to scorn.

The seventh hour so fast is gone,
over its use be torn
when the eighth bell is rung
day's clothes must we adorn.

It's known by now, the dangers
of which you never warn
as you said so stately
and thus this poem born:
*"Not nary a day goes by without my
tickling a buttcheek of your'n!"*

MY FAVORITE BOOK IS YOU

I don't need to turn your pages
to know what's written there
though every time I do
there's something new you share.

There's always more
or a paragraph I've missed
so I'll keep rereading until your soul's laid bare
and every word's been kissed.

Some passages I've highlighted
and fully know by heart
no longer dog-earing
like when we were apart.

Tightness in my throat
when Wendy grew too old
it's the same thing I felt at the start
when I read and did your words unfold.

Treasure Island, *The Great Gatsby*, and *The Book of Psalms*
when Tom signed in blood,
a knifepoint in their palms.

Familiarity,
the reason I slept with them abreast
the way your presence always calms
the tempest in my chest.

THE TRAGEDY OF LOVE

The world and its people once told me by example
a message in a blotch of inky cynicism:

Some men's tragedy is that they never fall in love
others is that they do
either way they pay the price
for what they never knew

The first kind of tragedy doesn't ache
it's just a little bit cold, maybe
I wouldn't know.

The saddest part about it
the tragic figure is unaware of his casting
looking on
thinking he occupies the role of a side character.

The wise man
or even the comic relief.

He will never know
he lives a tale more doleful than Romeo
and twice as incomplete.

But oh, the stricken ones who love!
The ones
who pull back the covers of their humanity
and say to another
Climb in.

We do not need to utter so much as a whimper for them
they know their predicament
dry eyes and grim smiles are more fitting.

I do not know much of anything
about what I have just written
but
if falling in love is a tragedy
I hope my life is such
as would make Shakespeare weep.

Acknowledgments

I wish to thank the many people who have been a part of my journey to create this book. To my family and friends who have supported me in this endeavor, thank you. To Mikel, who took my laptop and refused to give it back until he had read my poems: Had you not invaded my privacy with your love, this book would not exist. You not only have me for the remainder of this life, but my gratitude and respect as well. To the strangers who have left a lasting impression on me, thank you for being irreplaceable. You have forever changed me, and it is my greatest wish that somehow you should come across this book and see yourself in it. To the strangers I have yet to collect, I think of you often and with great anticipation. Without you, my future would be sorely lacking. Finally, all glory to God, who has created every stranger and yet knows them all.

Summer Collins is a poet from North Carolina. She has also spent time living in Colorado and northern California. Apart from writing, she enjoys people watching, hiking, spending time with her husband, and making friends with both humans and animals. She has spent much of her adult life working in the camping industry, something she is very passionate about. Summer is an avid collector. She hopes that the characters in her poems will make the reader feel seen, or at least will encourage the reader to take notice of the strangers who occupy our world. *A Collection of Strangers* is her first published book.
To stay updated on Summer's writing visit summercollinswrites.com

Luke Jetté is an artist born and raised in Gainesville, Florida. About 6 years ago, he realized he had a love for the arts. Through many online resources, independent study, and a couple semesters of college-level drawing classes, he developed his talents and now often does commission work. Luke primarily focuses on landscapes and architectural drawings, with a certain enjoyment for European architecture. He works with unique requests such as the ones found in this book, including people, objects, and abstract design. Primarily, his art is a meditative and introspective way to get out on paper what's in his head.

www.ingramcontent.com/pod-product-compliance
Lightning Source LLC
Chambersburg PA
CBHW072026060426
42449CB00035B/2724